Building on the Rock

A Biblical Worldview and Bible Survey Curriculum for Grades K–5

Truth

Building the Foundation for Life on God's Word

Student Workbook
Grade K

 Summit Ministries

Acknowledgements

Vice President of Publishing: Karl Schaller

Managing Curriculum Editor: Macki Jones

Authors
John F. Hay, Jr.
Hannah Weber
Kim Pettit
Lorraine Wadman
Macki Jones
Nancy Sutton

Editorial Team
Hannah Weber
Janice Giles
Kim Pettit
Lorraine Wadman
Macki Jones

Illustrator
Aline Heiser

Design Team
Claire Coleman
ZignGuy Graphic Design

Worldview Model Design
Randy Bounds
Steven Myasoto

Published by Summit Press, P.O. Box 207, Manitou Springs, CO 80829

First Printing 2019
Printed in India

ISBN-13: 978-0-936163-84-0
ISBN-10: 0-936163-84-4

Building on the Rock Table of Contents—Student Workbook

Name

1. Color the ground that Wise William built his house on 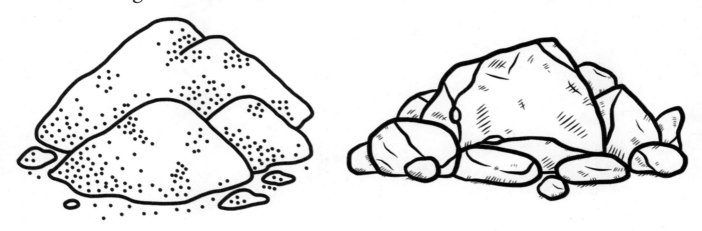. Color the ground Foolish Fred built his house on .

2. Make a line from Wise William to his house after the storm. Make a line from Foolish Fred to his house. Color the pictures.

Name

1. Jack and Jon are twins. Circle the twin who is reading God's Word.

2. Color the pictures to show where we get wisdom.

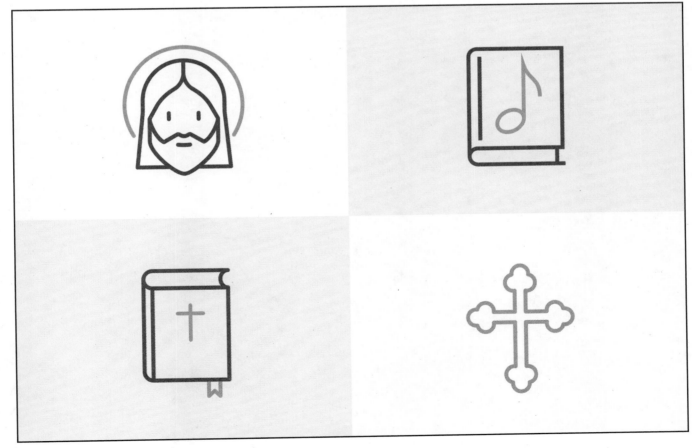

Name

Fill in the circle near the picture that shows a teacher reading the truth from God's Word. Make an **X** in the circle by the teacher who is reading a make-believe story.

Name

Count and write the number of boys and girls. Color the picture.

Boys _____   Girls _____

Name

1. Foolish Fred believes there should be more than one god. Circle what Wise William would say.

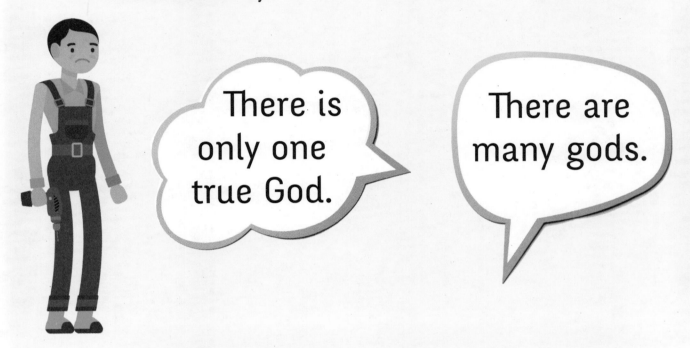

2. Color the spaces with the number 1 to reveal a truth about God.

Name

1. There is no place that God cannot be. Draw a line from the word to the image that matches it.

Classroom ●

House ●

Church ●

Library ●

●

●

●

●

2. Where else can God be? Draw a picture to show somewhere else that God can be.

Name _____

God uses people to show us his love. When we show love to others, we are sharing God's love. Draw a ♡ underneath each picture that shows love.

Name

1. Circle the picture of a father protecting his child.

2. Circle the picture of a father helping and teaching.

3. Circle the picture of a father making things.

4. God the Father provides for our needs. Circle our needs.

Name

Draw a line from the sentence to the picture that matches it.

1. Jesus was a teacher.

2. Jesus was a healer.

3. Jesus was a helper.

Name

1. Color the spaces with the letter B.

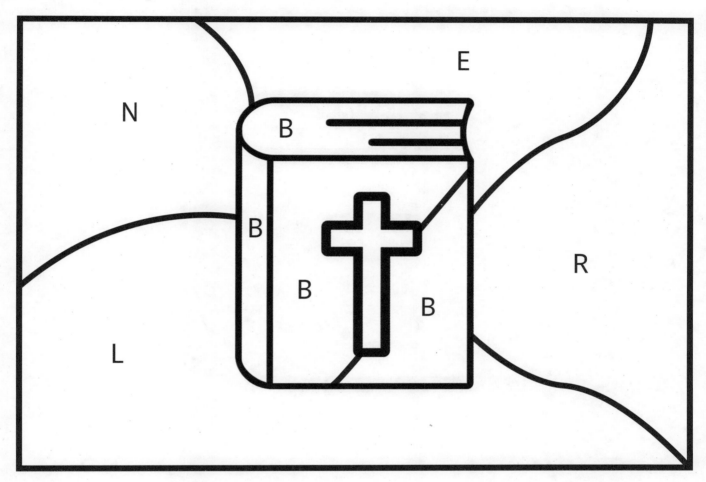

God the Holy Spirit helps us know the truth.

2. Trace the words to answer the question.

Who helps us know the truth?

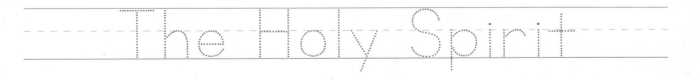

Name

God is three Persons in one. Count each group and circle the sets of three items.

Name

Cut out four things that God created and glue them in the sky.

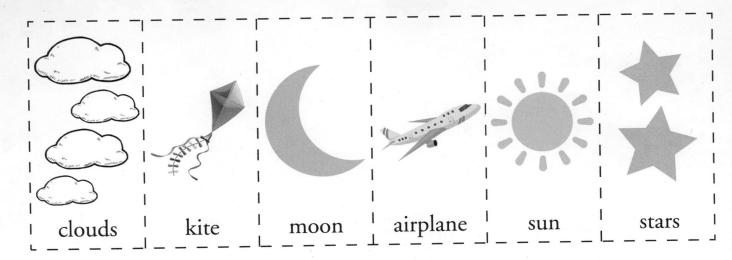

| clouds | kite | moon | airplane | sun | stars |

Name

1. Color the land green and the oceans blue.

2. Trace the words.

God made oceans and land

Name

1. Connect the dots from number 1 to 15.

2. Count the number of apples on the tree and write the number. _____

3. Trace the word.

God made plants.

Name

Use a ▬▬▶ to circle the things that God made and a ▭▬ to circle the things that people made.

Name _____

1. God made us for his pleasure. What can you make? Draw a line from the material to the art made from it.

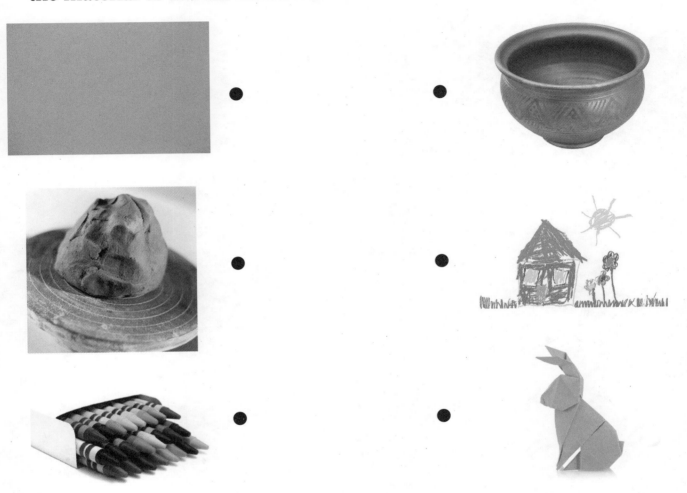

2. Jana made something for her friend. Circle what she made.

Name _____

1. God made people to grow in families. Circle the younger child. Make a line under the older child.

2. Circle the taller child.

3. The boy is growing up. Number the pictures in order from his birth.

_____   _____   _____   _____

Name

1. Make a line under the things God knows about you.

My feelings

My wishes

My thoughts

2. Make a line under the gifts of God that show his care for you.

My parents

My teacher

My bedroom

Name

God wants us to have peace with him, with ourselves, with others, and with the earth. Cut out the puzzle pieces. Make the puzzle.

Peace in My Heart

Peace with the Earth

Peace with Others

Peace with God

Name

1. God gives us and all creatures life. Circle the pictures that show things that are alive.

2. God gives us what we need to grow. Fill in the circle under the things we need to grow.

Name

1. God knows our needs. He knows we need comfort, friendships, and peace. Circle the picture that shows a parent comforting a child.

2. Circle the picture that shows friendship.

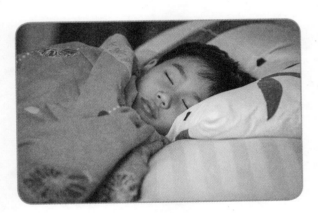 

3. Circle the picture that shows a peaceful child.

Name _____

1. God protects us. He gives us helpers to keep us safe. Fill in the circle of the people who help keep us safe.

2. Make an **X** in the box with objects that are keeping the child safe.

Name

1. God gives us minds to be able to make choices. In the story "Rudy Changes His Mind," Rudy was able to choose a pet. Draw a △ around the pet Rudy chose.

2. Find each **g**, **m**, and **w** in the sentences. Trace them.

God gave me a mind to think. God gave me a will to choose.

Name

1. Circle the emotion you should feel after you have sinned.

2. Trace the words at the top of each box. Then cut and glue the pictures that show sin and not sin.

sin	not sin

Name

Listen as the following scenarios are read aloud. If the scenario shows the sin of selfishness, circle the fish. If it shows lying, circle the lion.

1. Foolish Fred told Wise William that he left the hard hat at the construction site.

2. Wise William did not want to lend his hard hat to Foolish Fred.

3. Anthony told his mom he cleaned his room, but he had not cleaned it.

4. Sasha kept all the crayons to herself when she was coloring with her cousin.

5. Jaylen interrupted his dad while he was having a conversation.

6. Avery blamed her brother for a mess that she made.

Name _____

Fill in the circle that tells how you will be obedient.

I will be obedient by...

1.
○ doing my work neatly.
○ doing my work carelessly.

2.
○ throwing a temper tantrum.
○ doing what I am told with a good attitude.

3.
○ following directions the first time they are given.
○ following directions when I feel like it.

4.
○ following all of the classroom rules.
○ following only the classroom rules that I like.

5.
○ being kind.
○ being impolite.

6.
○ interrupting others when they speak.
○ using my manners.

Name

1. Color the picture according to the key to reveal what separates us from God.

Key

| 1 – |
| 2 – |
| 3 – |

2. God hides his face because he does not like to look at sin. Mark an **X** over the things that God hides his face from.

Name

1. Who is the bridge between God and people? Trace the answer.

God   Jesus   people

2. Cut out the pictures of Emmy and her daddy. Glue Emmy where the bridge begins. Glue her daddy at the end of the bridge.

Name _____

1. Fill in the circle below the picture that shows Justin taking Dylan's punishment.

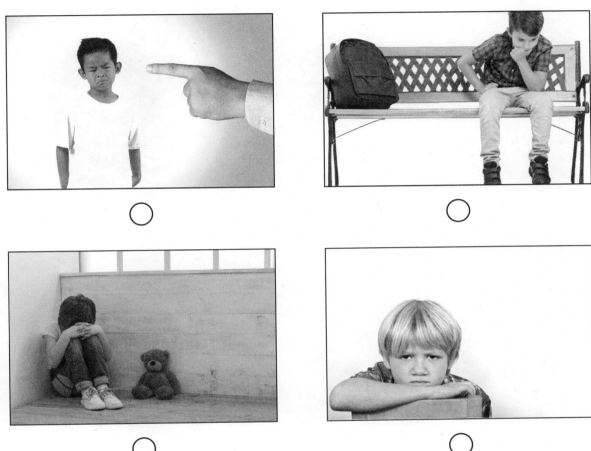

○   ○

○   ○

2. Fill in the circle below the picture that shows Jesus taking our punishment.

○   ○

Name

1. Make a ♡ next to each child who is praying for forgiveness.

Dear God, I am
sorry for my sins.

Dear God, please
forgive me.

Dear God, I
would like a pet.

Dear God, please
keep me safe.

2. Underline the picture that shows a child who has been forgiven.

Name

God wants to forgive our sins and make our hearts clean. If the sentence shows a forgiven heart, circle the clean heart. If the sentence shows an unforgiven heart, circle the dirty heart.

1. Jack took a cookie and lied about it. He was not sorry that he took the cookie.

2. Kelly felt sorry for being mean to her friend and asked God to forgive her.

3. Sam was sent to his room for disobeying. He pouted and was not sorry for his sin.

4. Tim had been selfishly watching his favorite television shows all evening. When he went to his room, he told God that he was sorry for how he had acted.

5. Maddy the Magician knows who can make our sins disappear. Color the letters E, S, U, J. Can you read the word?

Name _____

1. Find and circle the differences between these pictures.

2. Circle what is made in God's image.

3. Which is one way we are made in God's image? Check the box.

Name

Color the emoticon to show how you would feel in each situation.

Name _____

Fill in the circle to show what choice you would make.

1.

     ○   ○

2.

     ○   ○

3.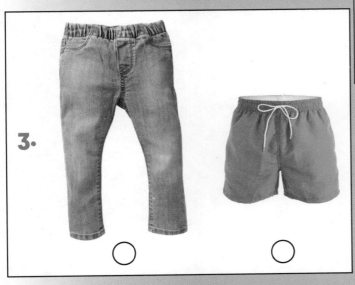

     ○   ○

4.

     ○   ○

5.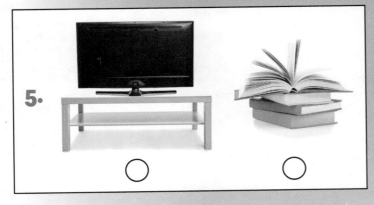

     ○   ○

6.

     ○   ○

Name _____

Cut out and glue into the heart the pictures that show right choices.

Name

A good way to honor others is by using good manners. Color the crown if the action shows good manners.

1. John says "thank you" to the person who held the door open for him.

2. Ralph let an elderly woman sit in his seat on the bus.

3. Riley took a piece of cake without asking first.

4. Amelia wrote a thank-you note to everyone who gave her a birthday gift.

5. Beth says "please" before asking for things.

6. Trudy cut in line because she wanted to be first.

7. Trace the words.

God gave people a crown of honor.

Name

Match the gemstone to the picture it represents.

1. We are to care for the earth.

2. We are made in God's image.

3. We have eternal life.

4. We have fellowship with God.

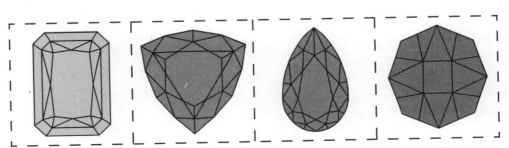

Name

1. Draw a picture of yourself and a picture of your partner.

Circle yes or no for each question.

2. God made people all the same.   Yes   No

3. God made people all different.   Yes   No

4. God gave a crown of honor only to tall people.   Yes   No

5. God loves everyone.   Yes   No

Name

God gave people authority over creation. Draw a line to match the person's job with the object that God created.

1.

2.

3.

4. Draw a crown around the crown of God's creation.

Name

Children are sometimes afraid when they sin. Put an **X** under the boy if the child in the story is afraid because of sin. Put an **X** under the girl if the child in the story is not afraid.

1. Jay took a cookie and worries that Mom will be mad.	
2. Jeannie did not ask for permission to watch a TV show. She is nervous because her Dad may find out.	
3. Amy helped her friend make an art project.	
4. Ted disobeyed his teacher. He is frightened that he will be punished.	

5. Match the sentence with the correct picture.

When I sin, I should
tell God I am sorry. •

When I sin and hurt my friend,
I should tell my friend I am sorry. •

Name

Bella has bad feelings in her heart because of her sin. Who can help Bella with these feelings? Complete the maze.

Name

1. Make an **X** through the children who are sinning. Make a ☐ around the children who are doing right.

2. Make an **S** under the children who are sad because of their sin. Make an **F** under the picture that shows a child asking for forgiveness.

Name

Color only the fruit of the Spirit.

love

joy

peace

selfishness

kindness

goodness

faithfulness

gentleness

anger

Name

Use a ▬▶ to circle things that make you happy. Use a ▬▶ to circle what gives you true happiness.

Name _____

1. Cut out the puzzle pieces below. Glue them in the correct order.

2. Circle the picture that represents peace. Cross out the picture that represents sin.

3. Trace the word.

Jesus   (peace. gives   Only

Name

When we believe in Jesus, he gives us a new heart. This new heart wants to please God. Color the heart under each picture that shows an activity that pleases God.

Name _____

Draw a line from the picture to the fruit of the Spirit that each child needs to grow in.

- kindness

- joy

- patience

- self-control

Name

1. Point to each word in Biblical Truth 13 as it is read.

God created people to love each other.

2. Fill in the missing words to Biblical Truth 13.

_____ created people

to _____ each other.

3. Color the picture. Answer the question.

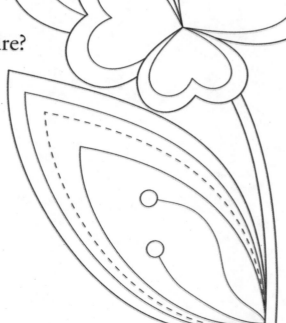

How many hearts are in the picture?

_____

Name

Help the girl get back to her mom. Read the words. Use a
to color the squares with the word **love**.

love	love	ten	sit	bag
jog	love	pig	see	like
home	love	love	love	six
hug	come	like	love	you
like	you	from	love	love

Name

Draw pictures in each of the circles of different types of gifts God gives.
Write the word on the line underneath.

Name

Color the heart if the action shows love.

1. Holding the door open for someone

2. Helping your dad clean the garage

3. Pouting because you did not get your way

4. Helping a boy who fell on the playground

5. Pushing someone because he or she made you mad

6. Cleaning up after you made a mess

7. Saying "please" and "thank you"

8. Being kind to a new student in class

9. Laughing at someone who tripped and fell

Name

Draw a picture of each person in your family. Write the name of each family member below his or her picture.

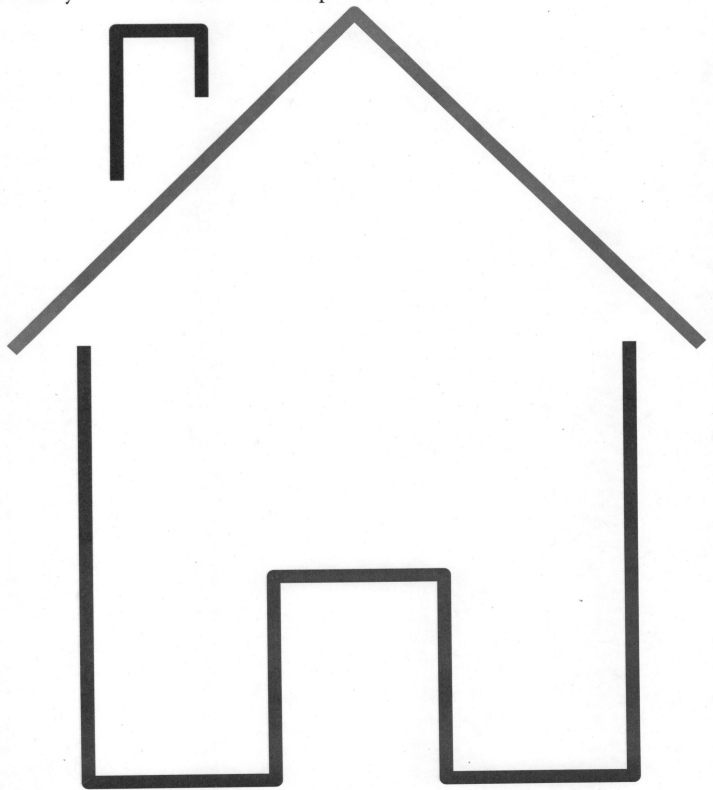

Name

Fill in the circle below the pictures that show the responsibilities God gave parents.

Name

1. Fill in the circle below the pictures that show the responsibilities God gave children.

Listening
◯

Bringing joy to your parents
◯

Obeying
◯

Obeying without complaint
◯

2. Whom should you obey? Fill in the missing letters.

G____d   D____ddy

M____mmy

Name

1. God planned for families to grow. Many families form communities, towns, and cities. Number the pictures from 1 to 4 beginning with the smallest community.

_____

_____

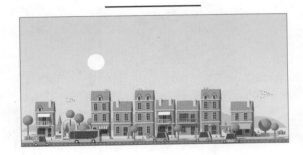

_____

_____

2. Count the houses and write the number on the line. Color the town.

_____

Name _____

1. Which seeds should you grow in your heart to be more like Jesus? Draw a 😊 in the circle next to the pictures of good seeds and a 🙁 by bad seeds.

2. Daniel wanted to ride his bike after he got home from school. His mom said that he had to clean his room and do his homework first. Daniel was upset and hid in his room instead of doing what his mom told him to do.

Number the pictures to show what Daniel should do to obey his mom.

_____ _____ _____

Name _____

1. Connect the dots from number 1 to 19. What did Esau trade his birthright for?

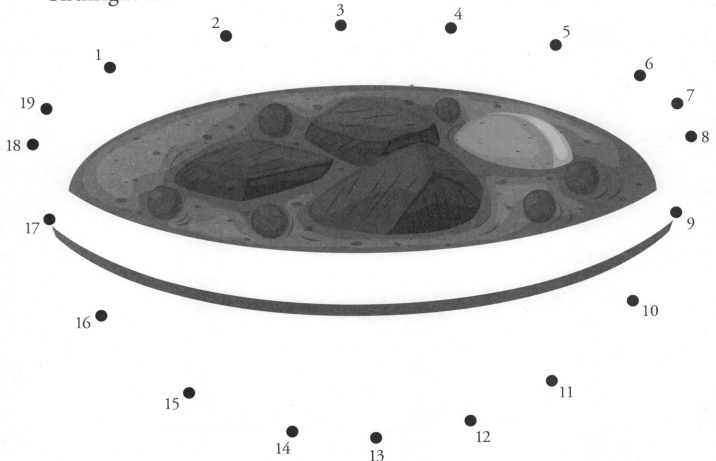

Circle the picture that answers each question.

2. Where does sin grow?

3. What does sin do to families?

Name

Cut and glue the words in the boxes to complete a prayer to God. Read the prayer with your teacher.

Dear God,

Help me [_____] , [_____] ,

[_____] , and

[_____] .

Thank you,

_____

_ _ _ _ _ _ _ _ _ _ _ _ _ _ _ _ _ _ _ _

get along with others

share

tell the truth

be kind

Name

Color the fruit that help you become more like Jesus. Mark an **X** on the fruits that caused problems between the villagers.

Name _____

1. Use the Word Bank to fill in the missing words.

Word Bank
God   family

Who is the Church?

The _____ of _____ .

2. Draw yourself and your family inside the church building. Color the picture.

Name _____

Draw a triangle around the items that represent Pentecost.

Name

Many people serve in the church. Write the number of the picture on the line to match the job.

_____ Worship leader

_____ Sunday school teacher

_____ Pastor

_____ Greeter

_____ Church secretary

_____ Janitor

Name _____

Cut out the pictures. Glue the matching picture in the correct square.

I can serve others.

I can teach others.

I can give gifts to others.

I can encourage others.

Name

1. Say the Biblical Truth 17 couplet with your teacher. Underline the rhyming words.

> God holds the earth together in his hand.
>
> Without his mighty power, it could not stand.

2. What does God hold together in his hand? Circle the answer.

3. The order of the seasons is one way God takes care of his creation. Cut out the pictures of the seasons, then glue them in order. Begin with winter on the top.

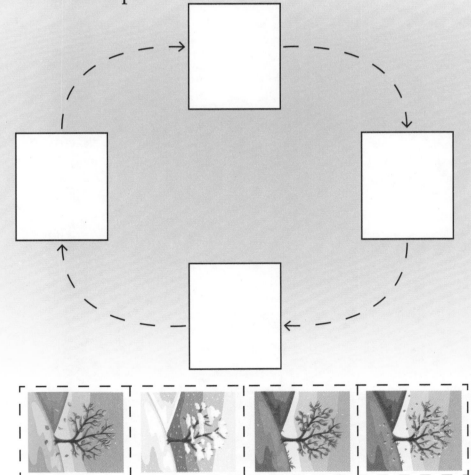

Name

1. Draw a line from the apple tree to the things that God gives it in order to grow.

2. Who provides what a plant needs in order to grow? Write your answer on the line.

Name

Match the animal to how God provides for it. Write the correct letter on the line. The first one is done for you.

1. ___B___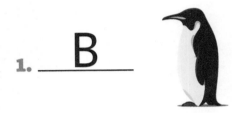

A.

2. _____

B.

3. _____

C.

4. _____

D.

5. _____

E.

6. Who takes care of animals? Circle every other letter to find the answer. Write the word on the line.

G E O N D R

_____

_____

Name

1. Use a ▭▶ to circle living things. Use a ▭▶ to circle nonliving things. Underline things humans need to live.

What are some ways God takes care of people? Make an **X** in the correct column.

	Yes	No
2. God gives people food.		
3. God provides water for us to drink.		
4. God tells us to sin.		
5. God gives people shelter.		
6. God gives people a mind to think.		
7. God doesn't help us make decisions.		

Name

Hillary and Charlie are caring for the earth by picking up trash. Help them make their way through the maze to the trash can.

Name

Circle the pictures of kids who are taking care of the earth.

Name

Listen to the story. Circle the answer to each question.

> Avery got a cat for her sixth birthday. She named her Lilly. Her mother told her that she had to care for Lilly every day. Every morning she had to fill up Lilly's food and water bowl. On Tuesdays, she had to clean Lilly's litter box. On Wednesdays, she had to brush Lilly. Every night, Avery had to make sure Lilly was asleep in her bed.

1. How did Avery care for Lilly every morning?

2. How did Avery care for Lilly every night?

3. How did Avery care for Lilly on Tuesdays?

4. How did Avery care for Lilly on Wednesdays?

Name

1. Replace the symbols with the letters to find out what God wants us to do.

A   K   O   R   T

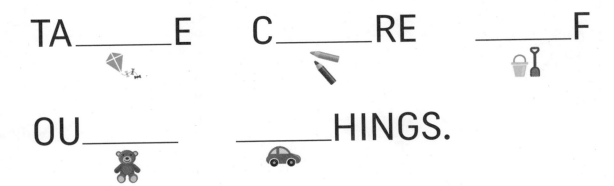

TA____E   C____RE   ____F

OU____   ____HINGS.

2. Circle the pictures that show someone being responsible.

Name

Circle yes or no to tell if the child took good care of the things pictured.

1.    Yes   No

2.    Yes   No

3.    Yes   No

4.    Yes   No

Name _____

Godly caretakers help the earth. Color the earth if the child is doing something to be a good caretaker.

Name

Godly caretakers help animals. Color the earth if a child is being a good caretaker of an animal.

Name _____

God wants us to take care of our bodies. Write **G** for good caretaking or **P** for poor caretaking.

1.  _____

 _____

2.  _____

 _____

3. 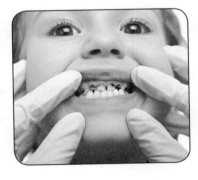 _____

 _____

Name _____

1. Write a word from the Word Bank to tell which part of creation has been affected by the sin of poor caretaking.

Word Bank
land   water   air

_____

_____

_____

Unscramble the letters to answer each question.

2. Who will make a new heaven and Earth?

_____

s s J u e   _____

3. What did Jesus do to fix the problems between people and the earth?

_____

e H   d d e i   _____.

Name

Draw a line to match the picture to Jesus' miracle.

1. Jesus healed the blind. •

•

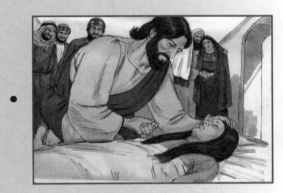

2. Jesus healed the lame. •

•

3. Jesus healed the sick. •

•

Name

Listen to the words that describe the New Jerusalem. Draw what you think the New Jerusalem looks like according to the Bible.

Name _____

Fill in the missing word to complete each sentence.

Word Bank

park   church   home   pet   bed

1. I can take care of my _____ .

2. I can take care of my _____ .

3. I can take care of my _____ .

4. I can take care of my _____ .

5. I can take care of my _____ .

Name _____

Cut and glue what God created in the order he created them.

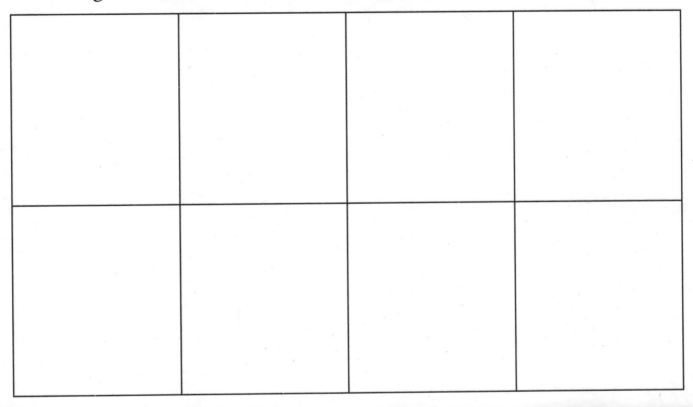

Name

1. Circle what God used to create Adam.

  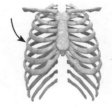

2. Circle what God used to create Eve.

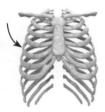  

3. Are all people after Adam created from dirt? Circle your answer.

Yes   No

4. Write the word **yes** under the pictures that show a way we are made in God's image. Write **no** under the pictures that do now show this.

Name _____

Cut and glue each picture to show how people protect and rule over each area of creation.

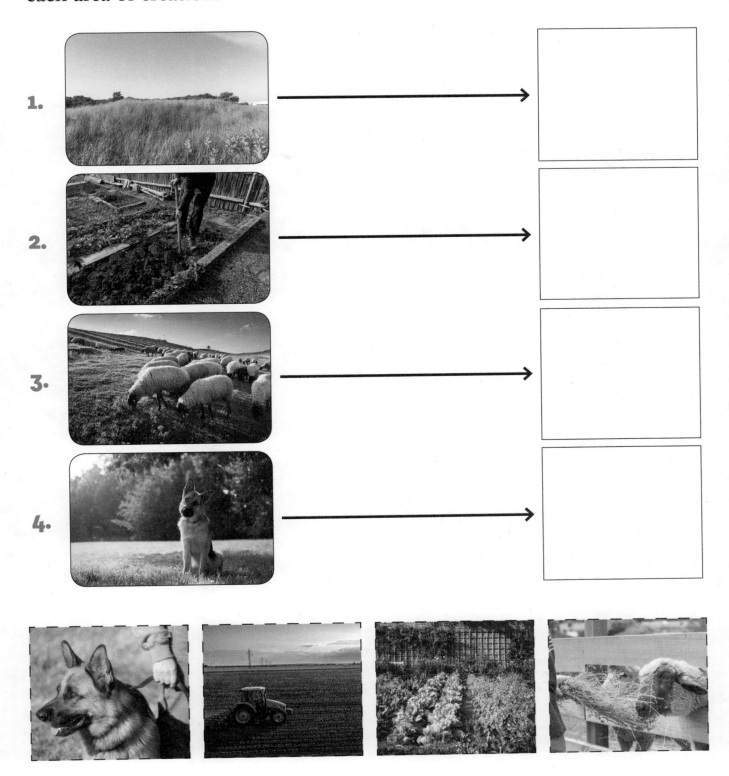

Name

Fill in the circle in front of each phrase that shows holiness.

1. I can have holy **thoughts** by …
○ being thankful for what I have
○ praying for those in need
○ wishing I had more toys

2. I can have holy **emotions** by …
○ being kind to my grandma
○ yelling to get my way
○ hugging someone who is sad

3. I can make holy **choices** by …
○ not doing my homework
○ doing my chores
○ cleaning my room

4. Who is making a holy choice? Circle your answer.

Name

Number the pictures in order to show how Satan tempted Eve.

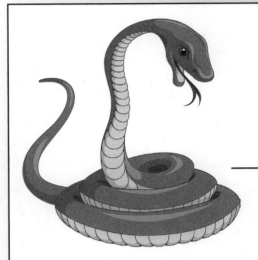

Satan looked like a serpent. He lied to Eve. He told her that if she ate the fruit, she would be wise, like God.

God told Adam and Eve not to eat the fruit from one tree.

Eve listened to Satan and ate the fruit.

Eve gave some fruit to Adam, and he ate it too.

Name _____

Write the words from the Word Bank in the correct places.

Word Bank
made   sad   hid   ate

1.

Adam and Eve

_____

_____ the fruit.

2.

They _____

clothes from leaves.

3.

Adam felt afraid and very

_____

_____ .

4.

Adam and Eve

_____

_____ from God.

Name

1. Adam blamed Eve for his sin. Eve blamed the serpent. How do you feel when someone blames you? Draw lines to match the feelings. Circle the word that tells you how you feel when you are blamed.

happy •   •

mad •   •

sad •   •

2. Sam and Ann blamed each other for not cleaning up. Now Mother is mad. What should the children do? Underline all the right choices.

Say they are sorry.

Clean up.

Keep blaming each other.

Name

Look at each picture. Circle yes if the child is using self-control. Circle no if he or she is not.

Yes   No   Yes   No   Yes   No

Yes   No   Yes   No   Yes   No

Yes   No   Yes   No   Yes   No

Name _____

Use the Word Bank to write the words about Noah or the other people on Earth. Write the words under the correct column.

Word Bank

ark   sinful   obeyed   wicked

Noah

Other People

Name

1. God told Noah to bring two of each animal onto the ark. Below are some animals that were on the ark. Write the names in ABC order.

dog

giraffe

zebra

monkey

cow

alligator

2. How many days and nights did it rain? Write the number on the line.

Name

Trace the path of the dove to reach the olive branch. Use the letters along the path to fill in the missing blanks to Biblical Truth 17.

_____ od _____ akes _____ are

_____ f _____ is _____ reation.

Name

Number the events from the story of Noah in the correct order. The first one is done for you.

	 The rain fell. 
	 Noah sent a dove.
1	The earth was full of sin. 
	Noah built an ark. 
	God made a promise. 
	Animals came two by two. 

Name

1. Find and color the words hidden in the puzzle. The first letter of each word is colored for you.

Word Bank

trust

Lot

Abram

tent

Sarai

move

t	S	A	r	a	i
e	x	b	z	w	k
n	t	r	u	s	t
t	q	a	m	x	r
a	z	m	o	v	e
L	o	t	q	n	k

2. Write a word from the Word Bank that best fits the sentence.

Abram had to _____ God.

Name

Color the stars that tell about God's promises to Abram.

 Abram's family would be as many as the stars.

 God kept his promise to Abram.

 God gave Abram a new home.

 God told Abram a lie.

 God didn't keep all of his promises to Abram.

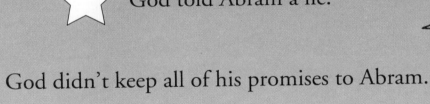 God guided Abram and Sarai to Canaan.

 God was faithful to Abram.

 God would make Abram a great nation.

 God did not bless Abram.

Name _____

Number the pictures in order to show God's promises to Abraham.

God told Abraham
and Sarah they
would have a son. _____

God told Abraham that
he would be a father to
many nations. _____

God gave
Abraham the
land of Canaan. _____

God led Abraham
to a new land. _____

Name

Below is a birth announcement for baby Isaac. Use the Word Bank to fill in the missing words.

Word Bank

| 90 | 100 | promise | Isaac |

it's a boy

_____

Baby _____ is born!

Daddy Abraham is _____ years old.

Mommy Sarah is _____ years old.

God's _____ came true!

Name

1. Listen to the story. Circle the words that complete the story.

Once there was a man named Jacob who had (10 / 12) sons. Out of all of his sons, (Joseph / Samuel) was his favorite. Jacob wanted to show Joseph how much he loved him, so he had a very special (bed / coat) made for him. It was very (furry / colorful). Whenever Joseph wore it, his brothers were (jealous / happy).

2. What emotion did Joseph's brothers feel? Circle your answer.

3. What does God want you to do when you feel jealous? Circle your answer.

Name

1. Fill in the circles of the sentences that tell about Joseph's dreams.
   ○ His brothers' bundles of grain bowed down to Joseph's bundle.
   ○ His brothers were happy for Joseph.
   ○ The sun, moon, and 11 stars bowed down to Joseph.
   ○ His brothers were more jealous than before.

Listen to the following stories. Circle the animal to show if jealousy or love was the emotion the child felt.

2. Jamie has a new baby sister. Jamie always feels that her baby sister gets more attention from her mom and dad.

3. Kallie got the last piece of cake from the table. When she noticed that Mitch didn't get any cake, she chose to share her slice with him.

4. Jordan always hears his friends talk about playing on their tablets at home. Jordan wants his own tablet to play on at home.

5. At the playground, Lena saw a boy fall. Lena went over to see if he needed help.

Name

While in prison, Joseph told the meaning of dreams. Cross out the image that does not belong in each dream.

Name

Color in the squares with the letters M, X, Y, K, and S. Use the leftover letters from left to right to find out the answer to the question.

Instead of taking revenge on his brothers, what did Joseph do?

F	S	Y	O	M
K	X	R	Y	K
G	Y	M	S	M
S	X	A	M	S
V	M	S	X	E

Joseph _____ _____ _____ _____ _____ _____ _____

his brothers.

Name

Find and circle: Miriam, Baby Moses, a frog, a cat, a lizard, a snail, a turtle, a bird, a butterfly, and a fish.

Name

Circle T if the sentence is true. Circle F if it is false.

1. God called Moses to free his people.   **T**   **F**

2. God said his name is I AM WHO I AM.   **T**   **F**

3. Color the burning bush according to the color key. Draw Moses' sandals by the bush.

Color key:

Leaves = green

Trunk = brown

Flames = orange

Name _____

Number the images in the order of the plagues.

_____ and _____   _____ and _____

_____ and _____

_____ and _____

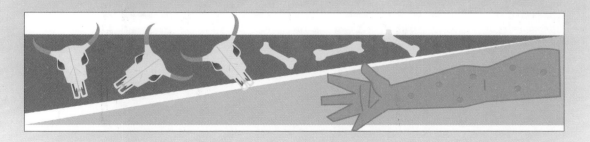

_____ and _____

Name

Circle the picture that best matches the sentence.

1. Moses went up the mountain.

2. A big wind blew over the water.

3. God made the Red Sea part.

4. God gave Moses 10 laws.

5. Moses led the people on dry land.

6. Moses gave the laws to the people.

Name

Color the footprint if the sentence tells a promise that God gave Joshua and the Israelites.

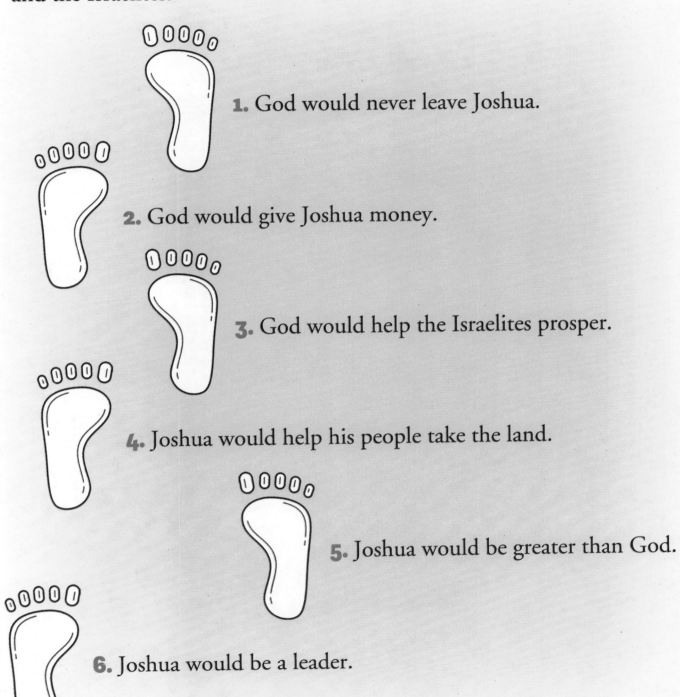

1. God would never leave Joshua.

2. God would give Joshua money.

3. God would help the Israelites prosper.

4. Joshua would help his people take the land.

5. Joshua would be greater than God.

6. Joshua would be a leader.

Name

Write words from the Word Bank to complete each sentence.

Word Bank
hid   sent   led   find

1.

Joshua _____

the Israelites.

2.

The spies were _____

to look over Jericho.

3.

The king wanted to

_____ the spies.

4.

Rahab _____

the spies.

Name

Help Joshua and his people enter the city of Jericho.

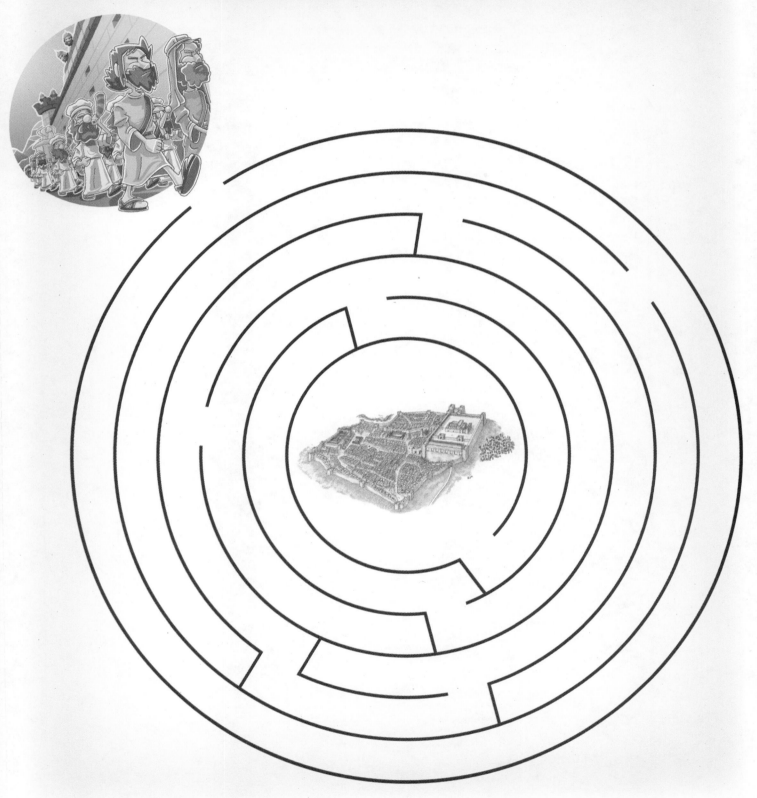

Name

1. Cut out the words and glue them in order to answer the question.

What question did Joshua ask the Israelites?

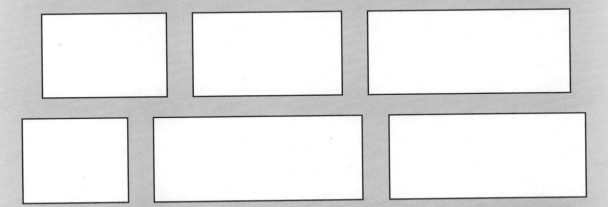

2. What choice did the Israelites make? Circle the correct word.

They chose to (disobey / serve) God.

to	serve	God?
you	want	Do

Name

Draw a line from Ruth and Naomi to each picture that shows loyalty.

Name

1. Find and circle the five differences between the pictures below.

2. Circle the character trait that best describes Ruth.

lazy   proud   **shy**   loyal   selfish   holy

Name

Put a check mark in the box by each item that is true about Ruth.

1. ☐ never married

2. ☐ stayed with Naomi

3. ☐ worked in a field

4. ☐ married Boaz

5. ☐ lived alone

6. ☐ had a son

Name

Cut out the pictures. On the bottle, glue the pictures of things you should be loyal to.

I will be loyal.

Name

Draw a shape inside the ☐ to correctly complete the sentence.

1. People look at the outside, but God looks at the ☐ .

2. Find and circle the following things in the picture above:

a shepherd's staff   David   six brothers   Samuel

Find and draw a triangle around the following things:

sandals   a horn   a sheep   Jesse

Name

Match the stones to correctly complete the sentence.

1. David   •   •   dared someone to fight him.

2. Jesse   •   •   put his armor on David.

3. King Saul   •   •   sent David with food for his brothers.

4. Goliath   •   •   were in the army.

5. David's brothers   •   •   trusted in God.

6. Circle the weapons that David used to kill Goliath.

Name _____

1. Jonathan and David were best friends. How should friends treat each other? Underline the words below the pictures of friendship.

encourage

apologize

love each other

share

work as a team

argue

2. Unscramble the letters f, i, e, r, n, d to write the word that tells about David and Jonathan.

_____

_____

Name _____

Write the long e word that completes each sentence.

Word Bank

meet   seat   eat   feet   mean

1. Mephibosheth was hurt in both _____ .

2. King David wanted to _____ Mephibosheth.

3. Mephibosheth was afraid David would be _____ to him.

4. David was kind and gave Mephibosheth a _____ at his table.

5. From that day on, Mephibosheth would _____ with David's family.

Name

Write **yes** if the statement is true about the story of Elijah. Write **no** if it is false.

1. Ahab worshipped false gods. ----------

Ahab worshipped the one true God. ----------

2. Ahab made God happy. ----------

Ahab made God angry. ----------

3. God caused a rainbow to form in the sky. ----------

God caused a drought to come to the land. ----------

4. God provided food for Elijah. ----------

God forgot about Elijah. ----------

Name _____

Reverence is showing respect for God. Each picture shows a child demonstrating reverence. Use the Word Bank to fill in the missing word in each sentence.

Word Bank
Bible   praying   singing

1.   I can show reverence by
_____

_____ praises to God.

2. I can show reverence by reading
_____

_____

my _____ .

3.   I can show reverence by
_____

_____

_____ to God.

Name _____

1. Cross out the words that start with the letter B. Write the remaining words on the lines below to answer the question.

bake	God	brown	by
answered	book	blue	Elijah's
boy	but	prayers	be

How did God respond to Elijah's prayers?

_____ _____

_____ _____

_____ _____

2. Circle the picture that best shows the way God spoke to Elijah.

3. Circle the object that Elijah put on Elisha.

Name

Use the words below the matching pictures to fill in the blanks.

 Elijah  Lord  cloak  fire  Elisha

 _____ _____

_____ wanted to serve the _____ .

 _____

_____ asked God to send his Spirit on him.

 _____

_____ went up to heaven on a chariot of

 _____ _____

_____ . His _____

_____

fell off him. The Spirit of the _____ was with

 _____

_____ .

Name _____

Follow the color key to color Mary and Joseph as they travel to Bethlehem.

1 = brown
2 = black
3 = red
4 = blue
5 = green
6 = tan

Name

Number the events of Jesus' birth.

_____ Joseph and Mary went to Bethlehem.

_____ Jesus was born.

_____ They stayed in a stable.

_____ The shepherds worshipped Jesus.

_____ The shepherds heard angels.

_____ One angel said, "Good news!"

Name

Write **S** if the pictures are the same for Jesus and for you. Write **D** if they are different.

1. Jesus grew up.

I am growing up.

2. Jesus learned to write.

I am learning to write.

3. Jesus' parents took him to Jerusalem.

My parents take me camping.

4. Jesus' parents cared for him.

My parents care for me.

5. Jesus shared God's Word with others.

I can share God's Word too.

Name _____

Circle the picture that best completes each sentence.

1. John was Jesus' cousin. He lived in the _____.

desert

rainforest

2. John ate wild honey and _____.

beetles

grasshoppers

3. John told the people to _____.

be sorry for their sins

talk to the priests

4. When John baptized Jesus, the Holy Spirit came down as a _____.

owl

dove

5. Christians baptize with _____.

water

milk

Name

Cut out the phrases. If the phrase tells a way to be a Good Samaritan, glue it in the box below.

I can be a Good Samaritan by ...

1. talking while others are talking

2. sharing   3. being bossy   4. loving my neighbor

5. asking if someone needs help   6. making a mess at lunch

7. letting someone else go first   8. taking a friend's snack

9. helping someone in need   10. helping people when they fall

Name

Find the missing vowels and write them in the correct spot to reveal how God feels about his lost sheep.

H__ C__R__S

F__R TH__M

Name

Draw a line to complete each sentence.

1. The woman in the parable lost a •

• happy.

2. When she lost it, she felt •

• coin.

3. When she found it, she felt •

• sad.

4. Draw a picture of something you lost and then found.

5. Circle the face that shows how you felt when you lost the item.

6. Circle the face that shows how you felt when you found the item.

Name _____

Use the Word Bank to find the word for each picture. Write it on the line.

Word Bank

money	ring	shoes
robe	pigs	father

_____

_____

_____

_____

_____

Name _____

Circle the people who showed love and compassion for others.

Jesus knew the people were hungry.

Philip worried about the cost.

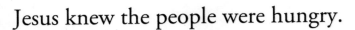

Andrew found a boy who had some food. The boy gave his food to Jesus.

Jesus gave thanks to God.

Jesus fed the people.

Name _____

Complete the story by writing the words from the Word Bank.

Word Bank

the   see   go   in   it   up   is   to   be

Jesus and his friends went to talk to _____ people. A man

named Jairus came to _____ Jesus. His little girl was very

sick. Jesus wanted _____ help. But someone came to Jairus.

He said the girl was dead. Jesus wanted to _____ to Jairus'

house. Jesus saw the girl _____ bed. Jesus said, "She

_____ sleeping. He took her hand. He told her to

stand _____ . She stood up. Her parents

could not believe _____ . Their

child would _____ well again.

Name

Cut out the pictures and glue them in the order of the story.

1. Jesus met 10 men who were sick.

2. On the way to the priests, all 10 were healed.

3. One man came back to give thanks.

4. Jesus asked where the other nine men had gone.

Name _____

Write the letter **C** below the pictures that show compassion.

_____

_____

_____

_____

_____

_____

Name

Fill in the missing words to complete the sentences about the time when Jesus entered Jerusalem.

Word Bank

Hosanna   palm   Sunday   donkey

1. Jesus rode into Jerusalem on a _____ .

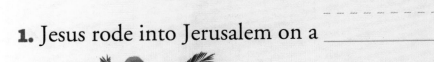

2. Crowds gathered, shouting " _____ ".

3. They waved _____ branches.

4. This day is called Palm _____ .

Name _____

1. Color the items on the table that relate to the Last Supper.

2. Circle the names of the two foods used for the Last Supper.

wine, or grape juice   meat   fruit

potato   bread   fish

Name _____

1. Use the Word Bank to find and color the missing words from Biblical Truth 8 in the puzzle. Then write the missing words on the lines below.

Word Bank

peace   God   people   Jesus

z	n	p	z	m	v
l	J	e	s	u	s
s	m	a	y	k	x
g	r	c	G	o	d
v	n	e	y	t	l
p	e	o	p	l	e

_____ died to bring _____

between _____ and _____ .

2. Circle the emotions that Jesus may have felt during his crucifixion.

3. Draw an emotion that you feel because of Jesus' crucifixion. Then write the word that describes your emotion.

_____

_____

Name _____

Fill in the circle next to each sentence that answers the question.

1. What news had the angels shared?
　○ Jesus had risen.　　　　○ Jesus had a brother.

2. What big lie did the soldiers tell?
　○ The disciples stole Jesus' body.　　○ Jesus had risen.

3. What did the women do when they saw Jesus?
　○ They yelled at him.　　　　○ They worshipped him.

4. What did the disciples do when Jesus met them in Galilee?
　○ They laughed at him.　　　　○ They worshipped him.

5. Circle symbols of Resurrection Sunday, or Easter.